Hide
and
Seek

LAURENCE KING

Published in 2015 by
Laurence King Publishing Ltd
361–373 City Road
London EC1V 1LR
United Kingdom
Tel: +44 20 7841 6900
Fax: +44 20 7841 6910
e-mail: enquiries@laurenceking.com
www.laurenceking.com

A catalogue record for this book is available from
the British Library

Design by The Urban Ant

ISBN: 978-1-78067-590-9

Printed in China

Hide
and
Seek

An Around-the-World
Animal Search

Charlene Man

Laurence King Publishing
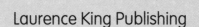

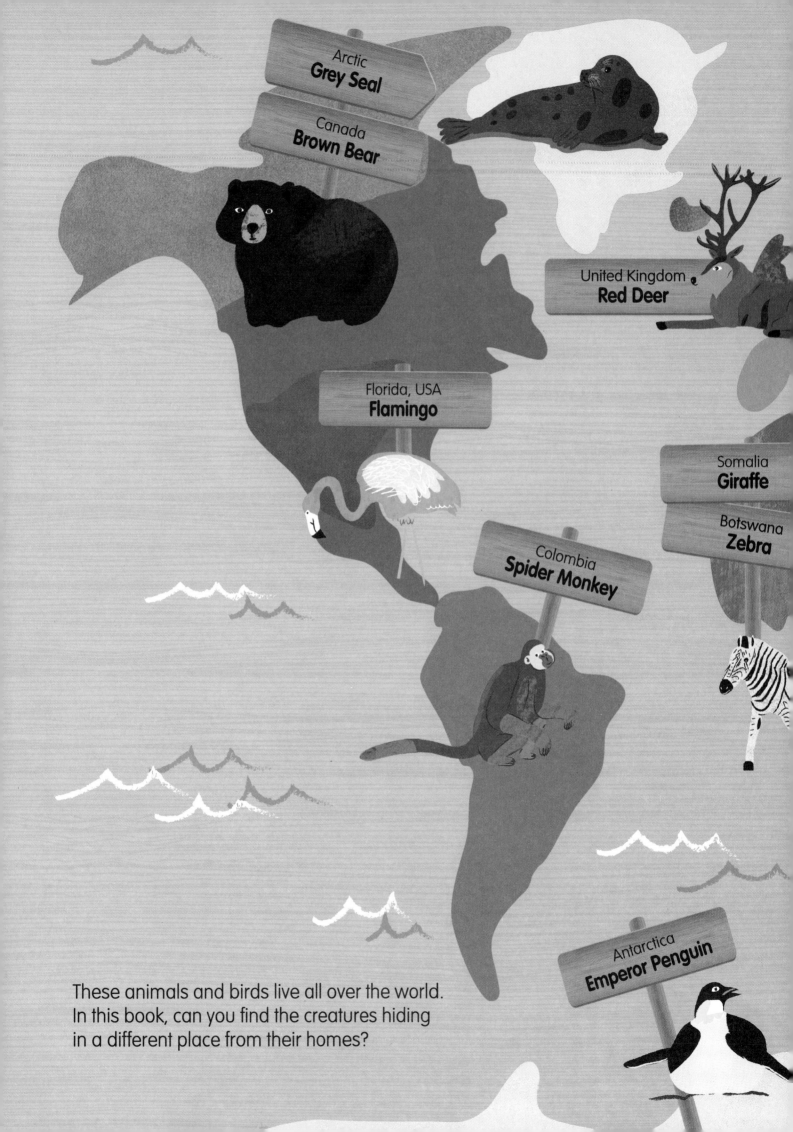

Arctic
Grey Seal

Canada
Brown Bear

United Kingdom
Red Deer

Florida, USA
Flamingo

Somalia
Giraffe

Botswana
Zebra

Colombia
Spider Monkey

Antarctica
Emperor Penguin

These animals and birds live all over the world.
In this book, can you find the creatures hiding
in a different place from their homes?

Watch out for those antlers!
Can you see who has arrived to join the red deer?

The emperor penguins are having fun in the snow.
Can you find their furry friend?

Koalas use their long arms to hold on to tree trunks high in the air. Who is also perching here?

Brrr! It's chilly in this forest.
Who is visiting the grey wolves?

Spider monkeys leap and dart through the trees.
Who is their slow-moving visitor?

Giraffes have a sunny home, but someone here has a thick coat to keep him warm in the snow.

Giant pandas are well known for their distinctive black and white fur. Who is their new friend?

You can't miss these bright pink flamingos, but can you see who has come to join them?

Grey seals catch fish and rest on the ice.
They've got a dinner guest who is used to dry land!

Brown bears enjoy playing, but they can't climb trees as fast as the animal who is hiding here.

Long-tailed parakeets eat fruits, seeds and flowers.
Who has come to join the feast?

Ring-tailed lemurs have long stripy tails.
Can you spot the odd one out?

Zebras gather at the oasis to cool off.
Who is used to much colder weather?

One animal is still hiding somewhere
in this book. See if you can find her.